"The work of Tony Brewer, while gentle and meditative, maintains a weight and impact that creeps up slowly. Humorous at times, without being silly. Serious, without losing its fun. A child discovering his mortality. A pistol at a poetry reading. The politics of shaving your balls. This is the world of Tony Brewer, and it might be your world too."

— J.I.B., author of AMERICAN TELEVISION

"Tony Brewer, an observer of the history of both art and war and a practitioner of ritual, constructs poems the same way others have constructed pyramids, tuned up trucks, or accessorized their human limbs. Here in *Good Job, Lightning,* he guides us through the psychodrama of parking lots and relationships, while steering us safely clear of bar fights, explosions, and the stomping feet of gods, and we will be better for it."

—Jonathan S. Baker, author of *Pressure*, editor at Pure Sleeze Press, and host of Poetry Speaks: Poetry and Spoken Word Performances

"The poems in *Good Job, Lightning* are understated ironic critiques of a surreal American landscape populated by a literalized back-alley arms dealer; giggling Dalai Lama acolytes; and an unhoused woman, who carries spare underwear in "a big bag full / of wrong chargers." Surreal vignettes alternate with tantalizing glimpses of personal experience: ghosting a wannabe Facebook friend; parking lot foreplay before shopping at Kroger; and the cathartic burial of a stolen pocketknife. Thus, the personal and the political are welded together throughout this collection—the undercurrent of memory being the lightning that does its good quicksilver job."

—Hiromi Yoshida, author of *Green Roses Bloom for Icarus*

Good Job, Lightning

Poems by Tony Brewer

STUBBORN MULE PRESS
DEVIL'S ELBOW, MO

Stubborn Mule Press
Devil's Elbow, Missouri

Copyright ©Tony Brewer, 2024

First Edition: 1 3 5 7 9 10 8 6 4 2

ISBN:978-1-958182-67-3

LCCN: 2024934932

Cover photo: Dickenson V. Alley ca. 1899

Author photo: Claire Mauschbaugh, manipulated by David O'Nan

Acknowledgments

Love & Deep Gratitude:

Marie Metelnick, Joan Hawkins, Eric Rensberger, Antonia Matthew, Kyle Quass, Hiromi Yoshida, Brooke Nicole Plummer, Reservoir Dogwoods Jason Ammerman and Matthew Jackson. Also Jonie McIntire, John Dorsey, Jason Ryberg, John Burroughs, Mark McClane and Osage Arts Community, Jonathan S Baker, and C.S. Mathews. Finally, Jeff Gburek, Brian Price, ORTET, Urban Deer Record Co., DREKKA and Imber Bright. You all have shared your many wonderful gifts with me, and I am truly grateful.

"One and Done" was written for "Disappearance," an online collaborative audio production of the Electroacoustical Poetical Society, mixed and produced by Marjorie Van Halteren. https://eaps.mixlr.com/recordings/2317523

"Real Deal" was written to accompany the collage "The 'Real' Folk Blues" for *Frames of Reference,* an art exhibition by poet Justin Hamm at The Hub Gallery, Rushville IL.

I am indebted to the Writers Guild at Bloomington, Bloomington Arts Commission, Indiana Arts Commission, Indiana Humanities, Osage Arts Community (Belle MO), and OAC Press for their ongoing support.

My thanks to the fine publications in which these poems first appeared, sometimes in an early form:

"Bree," *Flying Island,* "The Business End," "Home for the Holy Days," "Loving the Job," *Gasconade Review 8: Wolf at the Door, Nobody Home,* "Can you believe that shit?" "Parking Lot Autopsy," "Sexual History," *Pure Sleaze: Tickets to Midnight Vol. II,* "Corpse Flower," *Stormwash: Environmental Poems (*ed. Hiromi Yoshida), "The Dalai Lama Turns Seventy," *Stick Figure Poetry Quarterly,* "The Doctor Is In," *Live Nude Poems,* "Embarrassment of Riches," *Lothlorien Poetry Journal,* "Everything Must Go," *Of Rust and Glass,* "Fabulous Princess Trucks," *Mad Swirl,* "Grubs and Old Madonna," "The Illusion of Country Quiet," "My Condolences," *Linked Verse,* "The Guy in the Clutch T-shirt," *Trailer Park Quarterly* (text + audio), "Jetsam," *Red Wolf Periodical,* "Labor of Love," *Fevers of the Mind,* "Life Is a Race," *Up Your Ars Poetica Anthology* (ed. Susan C. Peters and Morgan M. Driscoll), "Noble Savage," *The Rye Whiskey Review,* "Petey," "The Politics of Shaving My Balls," *Bullshit Lit Magazine*

Table of Contents

For Jason Leslie Ammerman
brother of many stages
wooer of many hearts
blossoming dogwood
beside still waters
of the reservoir

Do you think loud orgies of luxurious good taste
can drown the moans of the tortured earth?
— Thomas Mann

That is the problem of silence:
one cannot test one's ideas.
Because they are not ideas, they are the truth.
— Louise Glück

I'd rather be a lightning rod than a seismograph.
— Ken Kesey

Everything Must Go

I went to the store the other day to replace my arm.
It had been hurting for a few months
and I saw an ad in a magazine about the new models
that can crush cans and slice tomatoes and julienne fries
like a Cuisinart and then retract and fold and hold
a child's delicate hand moments later.
I might like one of those. And the one I had hurt.
But the arm store was out of stock.
All they had were attachments, like aerodynamic elbow fins
and spindly fingers I know I'd snap off in a door slam.
All the salespeople had arms, of course, but they were no help.
I checked next door at the leg store
and those stilted cocksure merchants laughed
and said *What, you wanna look like a freak?*
They only cared about speed and shapely calves anyway
and I already got all that covered.
So I'm walking home dejected, unconsciously flexing,
when I hear *Psst! Hey, buddy, come 'ere!*
And there in the shadow of an alley stood an arms dealer.
And he was a good one. He said *I understand your predicament.*
You got money and demand. They got no supply.
It's a rough time now. Sour market. Bad economy. Caveat emptor.
The pit of his arm was whispering all this in my ear.
He had a nice, custom bicep. All tricked out.
I'll be honest, I didn't know arms could do that
and I had done a lot of research.
I allowed him to take me aside.
We stood next to a dumpster and a dripping water pipe
and he continued to pitch me appendages,

lefts and rights, though they all looked the same
lying there inert in his display case.
This one is for gardening and it has a power scoop.
This one can microwave — it's really really small.
Finally we got to a few that interested me.
One that could play charades with the other arm
and one that sprouted skin tags and moles and long
rogue hairs.
Very realistic. I liked that.
Arms with switchblade fingers and blunderbuss wrists
and extra elbows or quills for hair, eh, I don't know.
I really just wanted one that could hug
as well as connect my wrist to my shoulder,
and hold and touch, and lift and work my fingers.
You know, the usual. But without the pain.
I said *I can do all that now but it hurts.*
So I need a new, painless arm.
The dealer said *So a replacement, not an upgrade?*
Nobody does that anymore I guess.
Use an arm till it wears out
and then get another one just like it.
The guys at the arm store were shocked too.
As if I were trying to destroy their way of life.
I said *Yeah just an arm please.*
Just like this one. Like mine.
I don't want to kill anybody and I'm not into gardening.
The dealer said *You're one of those masturbators then?*
I could not deny that, but before he could
pull some perverted arm out
of that infinite case of his I stopped him
and said *I don't think you understand.*
My arm hurts but it's mine.

He said *To some people that's the only way*
you can tell you're alive. Pain and possession.
I said *You can't really show off an arm by itself though*
because it's attached to everything else.
He said *Yeah but these new models nowadays. Whew!*
If you practice you can detach them very quickly.
We went back and forth like this for a while,
in an alley next to a dumpster.
The pipe was still there but had stopped dripping.
Him trying to sell me arms I didn't need.
Me explaining why I wanted a new old arm.
You don't repair arms do you? I finally asked.
He laughed and said *Nobody fixes arms anymore.*
Profit margin's too low. Cheaper to junk it, buy a new one.
So I thanked him and shook his hand.
It was a really nice one but awfully flashy
and I think that's exactly why he had it.
Then I got out of there fast.
My arm still hurt but it was mine.
Everything stops hurting eventually,
one way or another.
I jammed my hand so deep
it ripped a hole in my pocket
and everything I had in there spilled
down my one good leg and out onto the street.

Corpse Flower

At 5 or 10 years old
a child realizes
his own mortality
at a family funeral
in line to touch grandma
one last time

Old men in dark suits
elephants grieving in a boneyard
I am lost among them

Years later
still lost among the suits
my impact evokes
a single Indian tear
the personal cleanup pact
sealed

Later still — too late
the bloom peaks — falls over
not dead but what
attracted and caught
innocent insects
with death stench
is a complex system
that feeds on me trying
to get out

Petey

There's only one Petey, thank God,
which is good because otherwise
Jesus would have to kill
all the other idols
and that's a lot of blood
on the hands of a mere god
even a bolt-throwing thrill-kill god
such as Zeus or one of those tentacled
Sumerian guys who hates everyone
and everything and one day will
devour us all

Petey says hard things, meaning
he has difficulty saying them
Petey could have nailed my sister
he was so hard last night
But he didn't
Instead he read about velour which
was a mistake and a huge turnoff
My sister is into raw silk and cashmere
Petey is a yard sale goldmine
my sister just drives right on by
She says she likes his stuff
She says, "I love Petey"
but deep down
she doesn't mean it
and she says it several times

Petey laments killing bugs
in his kitchen — but he kills
them anyway
He would never hurt anyone
or anything — the stomping
doesn't last too long
and he is very accurate
He likes his bug-covered floor because
he is above it and because
of the sound it makes
under his sneakers — hard-
wood, thumping, like a drum
like a heart beating
that stops when he's killed enough
when he's had his fill of killing

That's not really Petey
That's just me being weird,
trying to make him sound
more interesting than he already is,
which is hard to do
but not as hard as Petey.

The bugs mostly are ants
and Petey hears them scream
collectively, which may be why
he starts stomping again
Petey is not cruel or short-sighted, though
He is a giant and he towers
over hick poets and ants alike.

There's only one Petey, thank God.
I mean how many spliced haywire
clones of Woody Allen and Franz Kafka
can exist in this his perfect universe
at any one time?
More than one? I doubt it.
That's a lot to ask of Zeus
or even Cthulhu
though I'll bet he could
work in a little
immaculate Petey
just before his big
tentacle-laced Chuck Taylor
with a pentagram All-Star
comes crashing down
to the floor
above us all
THUMP
and that's it

I could listen to this terrible news forever

NPR in my face
and I didn't tune in
the tone of voice
that lets you know this
wounds me deeply inside
but we have to leave
it there, congressman
stand by for vocal fry
and a calm Cronkite on
gardening and astronomy
other conquered domains
orchestral music
quirky diversity
snark but gently gently
we used to ridicule grandma
tuning in like clockwork
to Lawrence Welk on Saturday night
such soothing inoffensive audio
now covering my face
down my own throat
I sound knowledgeable detached
as warm water splats and plashes
my body feels like dying
but brain chuckles lightly
leans into this
assured continuation

Bree

She openly admits she is codependent
standing on my porch in the dark
after Ray ran off with her clothes

A frantic knock at my screen door
a plea for my wi-fi
her phone dying
She had 2-3 years left
as long as she stayed clean
& she did through Christ
teaching her kids it's worse
if you don't believe & it's real
than if you believe
& it isn't

Eaten up by bugs
that don't bother me
she needs a ride
Ray says he's lost
Her thumbs batter the screen
What started as compassion
turns to OK get off my porch
her bundle of nerves
wadded up spare underwear
in a big bag full
of wrong chargers

But I don't crack
When she is calm she's thinking

of all she gave up to stay
for what felt like love
& it is

Two spirits fighting
to stay & to leave
rattling off the story
like a grocery list

Ray is waiting at the Exxon
nods when I pull up
She is jabbering furious
about what his fucking problem is
as her door opens
Dude looks tired worn out beat
by responsibility I claimed
for an hour of texting on my porch
I gladly turn over to him
& pull away

Jetsam

Three years later
she felt compelled to check
on me after the flood

I live on a hill & the cat
is fine I said — left it at that

I'm the survivor now
brave in the rain &
flinching at lightning — inwardly

Outside my favorite park
bronze lion statue
nose shiny from children
strong haunches splattered
with bird shit
greening mane frozen

its majesty captured forever
despite the waterline at
the soft white underbelly

Life Is a Race

My mushroom dealer in college
became a Navy JAG in S. Korea

Sweating behind dark glasses
at our table in the dorm cafeteria
he was sure he was going away
when his roommate got busted

He disowned us losers when he got in

My high school class president
friended me just to say #alllivesmatter
then vanished into the forgotten compartment
where I keep all those people

Mom convinced me I am going to hell
because some poems are critical of Dad

Wait till she finds the ones about Jesus

Happy Birthday, America!

Megan Fox has a weird thumb they say
I'd still put her feet in my mouth
after saving the world with robots

Every neighborhood is blowing up
with pyrotechnics & sirens for fires
All holidays are for assholes too

You can see in Witwicky's eyes
the trouble Shia will get into when he's older
but Meg loved him anyway

How our decadent god shapes everything
in the form of everything else
for convenience when we t-t-t-transform

Maybe something vestigial — a claw
she shivs a mate with after she comes
My cat thinks she can hide from it

But it goes on like this for weeks
gunfire the celebration at Qatar weddings
steely blue eyes against an orange explosion

Keep thinking evolution but machines are ancient
going back at least to the 80s
The Soundtrack of Car

Once you allow the little things
Slippery Slope City with junkyard rules
all sucked up into giant beams of slaves

Rising — someone lit a fuse so carefully
every explosion elicits mouths of surprises
You see them running in the dark — lighting

And then she's in my arms on a hood
The army freak-watches with metal eyes
No room for tools in this god's church

They're all monkeys with wrenches
keeping the last best American idea
made by Chinese children on the road

Movies drop like recruitment posters
pointing you in a direction
like a hitcher would with their thumb

Some Owners

The pistol fell out
of her jeans
at a poetry reading
Nice people
smokers
She came to spit
at the open mic
& he held it for her
She couldn't go
up there with it
armed when she wants
to be vulnerable
She kills it
takes the pistol back
when she sits down
He puts his cowboy
hat back on as they leave
us all appreciating
her commitment
to a revolver

There are many Krogers

Outer Kroger
Krogotten
The People's Kroger
John Kroger Mellencamp

across town
at Krogucci
a transitioning
cashier further
along on the journey

fresh brushstrokes
on a new painting

is the open human
I pick instead
of the U-Scan bot

I like humanity present
making efforts & working

on themselves like me

two citizens connected
through commerce

I help bag & mutter
have a good one
under black plastic

electric eyes installed
by corporate heads
who never

show their faces
around here

Home for the Holy Days

I try being smug
at the very real diner
thinking about my old haunts

Not this one
a new brewery sprung up
in my hometown

because every little town has
one it's partly why going
home is always weird

Back to not being listened to
Haven't done a thing since I was 12
My perfect silence

On my way "home" home
ambling into a non-Applebee's
experience for once

Treated like an old man
humored and placated
leaving a big tip:

Don't live so far away
you can't get home
when they need you
and realize sooner than later

they really don't need you

The Guy in the Clutch T-shirt

for Jason Ryberg

Somewhere between spicy IPA
& some flavorless Schlitz
a car is born idling both feet
ready to burn rubber — both pedals
options on the constant road

& the voice is a burnout
popped out of granny gear
all the way to red line
back to idle of repose

Can we start already?
or is this just where
it gets interesting
life by the metaphor
Racing stop to stop
the illusion of automatic
when it's all goddamn work

only the transmission
does it for you
in the barrel chest
of a mean street machine
running like a mouth
full of poem & spite

Racing & winning so far
ahead sometimes it feels
like living in last place

Fabulous Princess Trucks

On dainty neon wheels they glide
tractionless on skinny tires across
the gravel lot beside the grain elevator
Fairy godmother-conjured carriages
miraculously dirt-free & rolling coal
that could smell like jasmine

but it's just good ol' clean coal
& the air is thick with diesel clatter
Each coiffed manly royal steps
from their spotless 4x4 conveyance
ruggedly tousled & ready
for a night of quarter-mile cruising

Their love of ritual pageantry
The showcase of their art
just past sundown
like first stars at twilight
Their engine bays still grimy
motors running rich to smoke
& grumble haughtily
in contrast to the outer sheen

Old lady smokers fresh
from the beauty parlor bouffants
wrapped like custom fender flares
who never figured out how
to leave this town or why
when they own the humble runway
Tuesday nights right here

The Business End

I'm into war porn
know the models
by their payloads

When someone else does
evil when we do
it's unacceptable

I sound so political
as if saps sign up
because they feel something
wrong

Can you imagine
the might of an empire
agreeing with you
& vice versa?

But then I'm trained
to interrogate a country
not stare slack jawed
into the abyss of its barrels

questions answered by calling
History moments
the pendulum swings
right or left

always passing
through the middle
like a wrecking ball

attracted by visuals
titillated even
by a passion for machinery
the beauty of weapons

How could I resist?

The Dalai Lama Turns Seventy

and Bloomington is teeming with monks
across oceans and mountains they come
to great walls of cornfields

Maroon robes signify
limitless clarity only
knowing minds can conceive

Brown creaky leather loafers
black socks elevated to mid-calf
by samsara

Moving among merciless
children & wandering hungry
ghosts of Earth

they converge on greeting cards at Target
frowning, furrowing their golden heads
Erupting with belly laughs
reserved for such profane aisles

considering each card
whether his Holiness will get the joke
& moving on to another
perhaps more perfect
birthday blessing

My Condolences

I blew her name
writing it at
the top of 4 lines
wishing her wellness
speedy recovery
good thoughts &c.
on the way to Much Love
larger than my signature
crammed underneath
Cards seem soulless
but just look
at all these
hesitation marks
of deep concern

The Doctor Is In

Sitting in my car gloving up
before mask on to buy groceries

I'm in Mindy's old
Ford Fiesta — 1986 we're parked
in gravel between cornfields

her back seat jammed with wet
swim practice towels

as we navigate her stick shift
for a hustle in the front buckets

Gloving up with the news on
is Bon Jovi out of a boom box

because her car has no stereo
and every time feels like that first

Gloves snug as jeans
opening the nitrile cuff and inserting
my fingers bunched as bananas
flexing in ecstasy at the bind

carefully rough and excited
and scared and embarrassed

adding a layer of alone
is nothing like in the movies

her eager smile and that damp
hair in that moonlight

while at Kroger beneath the stare
of 360-degree surveillance lot cams

projected death tolls I cannot turn off
not feeling wild — wild in the streets

She guiding like a nurse
as I operate on a school night

with a playful snap of left glove
skin and breath weaponized

my bare fingers her anticipation
knees banging spasmodic against wheel wells

All survival acts should taste like this

I step out quiet in the populated void
onto the angled painted parking of a city

neither desperate nor essential
but still here and makeshift masked

bandana close as her mouth
wiping down the cart like a murderer
when once we were all over each other's hands

rolling bravely through the automatic
sliding doors into a touchable doom
where not a soul can see me smile

Grubs and Old Madonna

There's molting like grubs into larva
& there's the transmogrification of Madonna
Awesome in the classical sense
like a great naturally occurring granite edifice
weathered & scraped & rain washed
over millennia — seas go up seas go out
finally my eyes have evolved
rods & cones hyper-focused
by decades of art history
let alone patriarchal concepts of beauty
I drove 19 hours to glimpse a canyon
& it was foggy that day
It still exists
in my weatherproof sheltered mind
This ol' planet has seen some shit
still pumping out them ugly grubs
as if anyone besides woodpeckers
sniping them eyes closed
out of a dead tree
or mama flies
needs them to exist

Parking Lot Autopsy

At the parking lot autopsy we
discover origins in a dead bird
remnants after so much tread
enough to divine

Like a good OR
heavy metal on the stereo
too much urgency for gloves
we probe with consecrated
unsterilized sticks

Humans are not brutes
paleolithic operations prove
help existed a long long time
before the invention of red tape
sticking together this sad
excuse for an ark
bird after bird depart
never to return

as if we dumb hicks
might Frankenstein a pigeon
with our shock at complicated life
so unlike late night horror
we had to evolve
right there on the blacktop
to animate the animal
ourselves

Without Beginning or End

I wanted it to always be now
between me and you
— John Homan (1968–2023)

One poem opens like a gift
dissolves into another poem

mostly light & breath

this sun beautiful radiant
shafts through March clouds

even a parking lot looks
fabled capable of dreams

instead of chaotic stoppage

sun rising as it sets
sky a gradient of night

always on the way to dawn
his gifts dissolving into

another poem like breath

Throwing Out the Ceremonial Frog

for Brooke Nicole Plummer

Right in the moneymaker
of your tired eyes
from nowhere to
nowhere bound

Think of all the broken
parties in a lifetime
spent surviving the cop

of the inner worst critic
It takes mountains
to worry a river down
with your foot mashed

to the floor & the road
to someplace copacetic
opens like January blooms

Who lives in their scar
deciphers miseries & things
the writer dedication & things

Money makes itself
sick of satisfaction
what a gift!
so visualize your room
where to bend & how
to lift it

Sexual History

The glazed donut was invented
in 1803 by a ship captain
in New Amsterdam
to feed a crew of sailors
you can fit a whole one in your mouth
but have to chew to swallow

My dress code
requires attention to detail
such as (no) pants & (no) shoes
I work from home
in an enormous cube
greet political candidates
in my PJs & sex hair
They want my vote
I want to be needed
at my worst

I get turned off
by complicated geometry
the barrier of a consensual contract
love the sinuous curves
of signatures & the tactile
stimuli of paper & ink
numbed by legal consecrations
& torqued up by lawyers
in power suits

My gender nonconforming mail carrier
knocks when something won't fit
we've been banished from the polycule
to this godforsaken suburbia
where cules stay clothed
& kink is a produce aisle

I keep fingering my calculator
but the math will not behave
We are not jealous
but the need for multiples is fierce
does not subside with age
even after 4 hours &
the doctor has had a good long look
(mine in fact likes to watch)

Finally the server brings my food
with eyes that say is this
everything you asked for?
For once I feel like a tip
instead of dishing out the sting of rounding up
My favorite part? Signing my name bitch
& the little treats left behind
one for everyone involved
& nothing more

We Could Be Heroes

In place of majestic peaks
the highest hill in the county
surrounded by cornfields

No dragon but the dog
that chased me past its yard

Bullies ugly misshapen trolls

I built mythology
without epic tropes

A few years not eons
not good & evil
not even farm boy
turned knight

Farm adjacent
in orange streetlight

my sword Dad's pocketknife
I stole from his drawer
because I deserved it

& later put it
in his pocket
locked forever in his casket
armed against malevolence
snarling at the boneyard verge

or I just got tired of carrying
a grudge & saw & took
my chance to bury it
for good

Can you believe that shit?

Buddha has a clear stool
a lifetime of clarity
produces little odor
seated on a humble throne
master of his hungers
his colon smooth
no attachments
There — the golden gift
of his serenity
& powerful foaming stream
into the people's bowl
like all of life
flushed away

Embarrassment of Riches

Tearing into it
like a sloppy rib
this life I'm holding
so gingerly
to keep the whites clean
clothing I mean
& a flimsy trifold napkin
that should be a drop cloth
Fuck it
I chomp down
to the bone
& chip a tooth
smiling through gaps
dripping
marrow
wasted
I lick
the plate
clean

The Illusion of Country Quiet

broken by mowers
acres of unputtable green
A dually rumbles by
deaf driver turns up
the radio it's all
talk talk talk

my Uber driver eyes
me in her rear view
gigging her way out
of precarity
asks if this music is OK
I don't care
don't want to say
what I think about
anything
on the way to the liminal
airport terminal

but we chat about the weather

hot air blasting
out of long shafts
clears asphalt
everywhere
we are always
leaving or landing in
separated by thin
wild strips

Labor of Love

Maybe a way to build temples with all the wonder without
the slavery — though it has been debunked — that slaves
built temples ever — not slaves in our conception —
people who do what you say or die — more like wage
slaves — sweat equity investment — like the cutters
who had graduated high school and then straight to
the quarries — backs bent from decades of shimming
blocks — they stroll around campus with a sense of
pride — and relief — you could put kids through college
by building the buildings — at first a steady paycheck —
then seed money for that starter home — etc. — back
then such things were possible — now only imagination is
enslaved — builds no temples unless a J-O-B is attached
— imagine a church built on tithing *you* — no one would
pray therein — more a series of knowing nods as the
parishioners run their hands lovingly along the walls
— they'd just hire the lowest bid today — which is an
observation not a judgment — still well-built but corners
cut — people have unanswered questions — which is
why so many churches now resemble barns — something
raisable — can be put up in a day — belief the fleeting
commodity — always another brick — another swing of
the hammer — another day closer to paying off that debt

Loving the Job

My furnace guys jerk
each other around
friends longer than marriage
and they spar "like
an old couple" says Ron
I was thinking comedy duo routine
the artificial back-and-forth
of bickering without malice
requiring no setup
You know how this one goes:
old couple fighting
telling you it's normal
means they've lost the words for love
if they ever had them
Grown into the grade school
shoulder punch
Insults raining like tiny kisses
but an occasional peck on the cheek
Mom and Dad were like
nothing I'd ever laughed at
She hysterical in his
invisible stranglehold
while he bitched out her every move
Me in the belly of it
burning gently like a pilot light
That's how I relate to people
Are you serious or joking?
Did I buy a ticket to a show
or are we related?
Jokes aside they do good work
with one-year labor guarantee

Noble Savage

Bars are a bad place for a fight
sharps & blunts at every turn
as many enemies as friends
someone quick to call cops

Bars are a great place to start a fight
enough booze to drop the leash
dim details yawped above the din
pressure to push a brain to pull
another body into fists

Parking lots
the outside stepped into
dirty puddles
the only thing
quivering
at my feet

Real Deal

Got no sympathy for millionaires
cranking cranky old cars
to live a vintage sound
garage bigger than a juke joint
with a hired man to tune them

A muddy hand building mean machines
burning bills in the other
No — the mud comes clean
Crowns conceal the minstrelsy
like a shelf back of the shop
stuffed with awards
for finest portrayal
in front of specialized tools

Somebody's story somebody else ends
rocked into a chorus
egg hatching in my ears

The cry of whiskey pain
makes sense
the sweetness of its shape
Placeholder text
gulping down white space
& out comes pure tone gibberish
of old bluesman deviance
clearer now around the patois

Blues always a guitar
always what you always are
thief in the night & victim both
A crossroads bargain struck
The soul loses everything but music
the devil's record plays
on both sides

The Politics of Shaving My Balls

Go down on enough smooth strange
it begs the question — why not?
Well it's dangerous, frankly
I have emotional scars to prove it

Never tit for tat a woman, dude
know that a trimmed bush indeed
makes the tree look bigger
like a scared suddenly sky-clad mouse

With your sweatbox removed
lotta slippy slide going on
just sitting there in traffic
even imagining hearing the word
Kegel causes one to occur

You'd trim back your beard
if they asked — why not?
You'd bathe brush your teeth
shower shortly after pulling out

Mostly it's a feel & look
she likes no pubes in her teeth
I know — I've asked
gross personal intimate
& precisely the same reason
only a few crazy loudmouths
show up to hog the mic
at school board meetings
even though everyone has
the right to vote

One & Done

Lac Bataille / Battle Lake Suite

I fell asleep
in a Walmart parking lot
near the border
waiting for direction
woke up on a work crew of relations
rebuilding a deck in Quebec

Where I came from
veiled in your smoke
Can't see
but feel its presence

The fires aren't dying
so we keep it simple
with hammers
tearing out old joists
where pests have hollowed out
the center of pillars

The entire structure weak
& wobbly but you could still
stand on it & have cocktails
at moonset

There it is
rising over the trees
sinking behind the trees

There it goes

Old green slippery crumbling
faith kept 5 feet off the ground

40 years — 50 years

Obvious rot
where we tear at it

***

Mist on the lake
moving like smoke
Four super moons in a year
mesmerizing frog song
the wail of the sacred loon
woodpecker so bored
he's turned his attention to aluminum

Tell me the difference
I'll open the airlock
share this supply
We'll ride out
re-reconstruction
together

80 years later
not an end
an ending

Let's imagine instead
of the same ol' grim dark
this one proud nation
with a long tail
projected like different loving
strong as pride
stronger than realistic portrayals
of the dropping of bombs

Here's one from 80 years ago
with added sound effects
for gravitas

Contrails clear as cut marks
Blue eyes crying in the rain
Beautiful beautiful weaponry

We've all been there
The trick is to get out
without disappearing
completely
but get out

***

We did not get here overnight
acquiring something to protect
& swing a hammer so many times
the ring sounds out J-O-B

no retirement
no permanent vacation

just the skill of relaxing
bored into hustle
it hurts to sleep
hurts to eat the lovely animals
hurts me all the way back
back back
to the first meal
pureed & sweet

I take out my hearing aids
& put in my night teeth
& gulp it down
Young again any time I want
because old is forbidden

sounds like ice cracking
at a pouring
while ice melting just disappears
not a peep

Somewhere in there
make room for dancing
taken up with youth & doom
smallest fortunes wasted getting there
back back
to what already disappeared

***

Drifting
every little tadpole in the shallows
Remember the days
gone lead into gold?
I don't

Remember when sky was a pillar
universe danced around?
I do!
Remember me?
Remember me
I cannot go

Call it one end
one foreseen future
one & done

Rock solid
work over
Back at a border
invisible & open

I walk awake
through veils of smoke
strange worker on a family crew
enlightened like a haloed super moon
filled with bilingual nods

80 years later

Destined to fade
as melancholy as moonlight
heavy on a lake

Tony Brewer is a poet and audio artist from Bloomington, Indiana. He is executive director of the Spoken Word Stage at the 4th Street Festival and co-producer of the Writers Guild Spoken Word Series and the Urban Deer Performance Series. He has published 11 books and chapbooks including *Centaur* (with Jonathan S Baker, Dark Heart Press, 2024), *Fragile Batteries* (The Grind Stone, 2023), *Pity for Sale* (Gasconade Press, 2022), *Homunculus* (Dos Madres Press, 2019), and *Hot Type Cold Read* (Chatter House Press, 2013). Tony has been offering Poetry On Demand at coffeehouses, museums, cemeteries, churches, bars, and art and music festivals for over a decade, and he is a frequent collaborator with experimental music & field recording ensemble ORTET. Tony was named Indiana's 2024 Literary Champion by the Eugene and Marilyn Glick Indiana Authors Awards. linktr. ee/TonyBrewer

This project was made possible, in part, by generous support from the Osage Arts Community.

Osage Arts Community provides temporary time, space and support for the creation of new artistic works in a retreat format, serving creative people of all kinds — visual artists, composers, poets, fiction and nonfiction writers. Located on a 152-acre farm in an isolated rural mountainside setting in Central Missouri and bordered by ¾ of a mile of the Gasconade River, OAC provides residencies to those working alone, as well as welcoming collaborative teams, offering living space and workspace in a country environment to emerging and mid-career artists. For more information, visit us at www.osageac.org

Osage Arts Community